rosewater

ISBN 9798338127674

Cover art by Laura Makabresku
Author photo by Harrison McArtor
Edited by Stephanie Saywell

Contents:

For Lili.

"I was reminded of a painter friend who had started her career by depicting scenes from life, mainly deserted rooms, abandoned houses and discarded photographs of women. Gradually, her work became more abstract, and in her last exhibition, her paintings were splashes of rebellious color, like the two in my living room, dark patches with little droplets of blue. I asked about her progress from modern realism to abstraction. Reality has become so intolerable, she said, so bleak, that all I can paint now are the colors of my dreams."

—Azar Nafisi, *Reading Lolita in Tehran: A Memoir in Books*

golab بالگ

to make *golab*: fill pots with rose
the color of ill tongues,
distill water obsidian in inked soil,
and pour it over your father's grave.

to make rosewater: simmer petals
the way bloodletting
metabolizes dread
into a lobotomy of faith.
your eyes are smoldered candles
as you say amen
for the rabbi who prays for israeli soldiers.

to make rosewater: fear your brother's god.

centuries ago
iranians picked blossoms in song,
like the bloodshed of poppies
your father saw on the news.
the first time you saw him cry,
it was the scent of a mohammad rose.
before bouquets became blood clots,
before october the seventh,
you sit on an iranian zionism panel
defending his name.
glares are hypodermic vases
as your keffiyeh sweats.

golab is only pure before it sinks into his earth.

to make rosewater bitter:
diffuse wilting petals
picked from your father's perennials,
where alcoves bury earthbound lungs

the way kippahs slide off mass heads
and reincarnate into olive groves
paved and worn through airport security.

to make *golab* sweet:
use honey spat from bees that stung as a child.

you once knew the sweat of flowers as antiseptic,
the aroma of morphine and rose,
of gauze and veins
embroidered in saffron
when prayers perfume 42,000 bodies.
your father, alabaster,
making *golab* with poppies in his sleep.

there is a garden where lucid flowers grow from tear gas grenades.

how dare you use our name.

we tore the walls of auschwitz
and turned them into shrapnel.
missiles sing from shofars
as we rise up to kiss the torah.
arms stretched in prayer,
the way arms stretch to carry sons,
like mothers mourning
in a hell jews don't believe in.

we blink and unarchive a holocaust –
eyes turn to iron domes.
a star of david stitched as fresh veins.

gas chambers inhaled our breath,
now: exhale white phosphorus.
skies turn foil
as electric fences burn the sun.

ice cream trucks become morgues
holding smaller bodies
who used to chase their song
like the dawn chorus of pizmonim.
baruch hashem
fireworks taste like their intention.

yamakas stapled on scalps,
i shave my beard or grow it longer,
reaching mass graves of pomegranates
thrown like rocks against metal
or a fire spreading intravenously

you can't drown in the dead sea
where we float like martyrs

and feel the weight of the wailing wall—
torahs glued on bodies,
tallits cover mouths.
citing scripture, we hold illiterate hands.
shana tovah
i hope your fast means nothing.

i never wanted this birthright,
the privilege to print these words.

rabbi told me how torah pages tarnish from the oils in our fingers.
told me to hold a metal instrument to protect his words.
hold it like an airstrike.
hold it like your sister.
she saw god on mount sinai,
her back against the west bank.
her brother proposed to his wife on these same hills
and settled his love of an occupied heart.
now he falls asleep tense and impervious—
a victim of a faith destined to erase them.
say amen.

I woke up from a nightmare where I was trapped inside a synagogue. They wrapped my body in holy pages like a sarcophagus, and threw a match as I was burned with my religion. The fire engulfed mosques to an oil that burned for 75 years. Olive trees—a premonition of splintered limbs. Can you recite the Mourner's Kaddish for 42,000+ human shields?

in 50 years, the youngest child will ask why we did this
as we absorb her tears with a flag.
there are so many ways to smile during a genocide.

behind a glass at the holocaust museum lie
the shoes of 8,000 children. another ____
died this month in the name of our existence.
if only we could break the glass like kristallnacht,
but this was never in our name this was never
in our name this was never in our name
this was never in our name this wasn’t
in our name this is now our name this is
now our name this is now our name
this is now our name.
amen.

be patient with me.
it seems like yesterday locks of hair were microscope samples.
they searched for the rot of pineal glands
while we drank smoothies at corona del mar,
eyes coyly searching tide pools, murky and black.
therapist said: tape your tear ducts.
therapist said: amphetamines make you sleep.

they waited for tragedy.
phones rang as sirens from morbid poems found in
drawers searched in a butcher's rage,
turning the credenza to wood chips.

i never did see a therapist.

at newport we talked like a hacksaw
slowly chewing through glass.
beach flies luxuriating on algae –
i never spoke elegantly.   i didn't know how.
birth records were read inside quicksand,
oceans wet as cinder blocks,
negative or positive, I apologize for the inconclusive results.

it's true, I suppose,
pills electrified my bloodstream.
pot or adderall – the same.
synapses fry like *tahdig*
beneath richer rice   does it taste the same now?

in youth, I slept to avoid what felt like a brain aneurysm.
jogged in black plastic bags in a voltaic rage –
oversized shirts worn at temple,
or glued to skin at the beach   arms crossed over your chest.
matryoshkas lost in larger flesh,
there are so many ways to be concerned.

taciturn, the mark of the sadistic or drugged,
until centuries later we drink whiskey with propane lips,
ignite prior beaches in an ephemeral hug.

briefly, I lived here.

Shema

I sang shema every morning

in the temple without a home.

Now I cry along with the mourning

as the olives all turn to stone.

9

The Synagogue

I haven't been to a synagogue since October of 2023, but the temples appear in my dreams. I have this recurring nightmare where I open a Torah to pages of hostages who stare at me in a greyscale despair. Their crying faces are pixelated into a white noise that drowns the hum of drones. I watch an orchestra of victims painting stained glass as members of the congregation flood out in tunnels. They bore out chasms like ligaments and pile atop my body until I'm smothered beneath prayer. They demand to know: *Do you condemn our grief?* Livid men tear Torahs out of the triptych and lock me inside, the bibliosmia making me retch. A hand reaches through a fissure made in the structure, by who I don't know, and hands me the lipstick my mother wore at my Bar Mitzvah. I use it to autograph bombs. I use it to paint pride flags in Gaza. All the colors of the rainbow blind opaque eyes. A phylactery is lodged in my mouth, a pacifier nursing me silent at my father's funeral.

he saw how black mold responds to fire
that turns plaster spores into specters
of electric jesus halogen deities imploding
& salvaged in cellophane bags
to resuscitate wet records as found objects
orbiting his body from portland to san
francisco where the sky was a torn
canvas swallowing shelter

he saw how birth records respond to fire
his brick and mortar smile chiseled to gentle
permeance swaying through space
in burnt fabrics of moth wings in exile
that imprint home as a material decision
to ~~leave~~ stay succulents require less
water to survive

he saw how memories respond to fire
zedekiah king of judah before his home
catched spines falling into question mark
embers on art through a series of doorways
entered as vagabonds like amnesia skies
are easily removable

of landlords & arsonists
earthen in insufferable ash that stains
sutures in burnt espresso and shaving
beard hair on blank kodachrome prints
of ceilings opened to a cyanotype floor
as a mosaic of split fates he saw how fire
responds to us

cue arabic choir distorted in synth / roll six minute imperial prelude / tinge film the hue of dessert-stained shawls / too dark / pan camera on morally conflicted savior / ben affleck is at the peak of his career / cast shadows on bazaar scene extras / zoom in on the foreigners / can you make your eyes look more shifty / stain the lens with the filth of the shaw / source tanned whites to play ethnically vague villains / tell makeup to darken their skin / center camera on sympathetic iranian / cut / tell her to wrinkle her shawl until it's oppressed / action / we need an ayatollah who looks like jafar / roll john goodman laughing for comic levity / make him grow mutton chops! / the house we built is a parody of sanctions / zoom out / insert beheading scene after uprising sequence / too dark / remove this scene / edit lighthearted hollywood party montage / add 70's american rock for irony / marketing says the iranian audience loves whimsy / producer says bryan cranston will salvage u.s. iranian relations / play for first generation youth as history lesson / make them feel washed of their ancestry / make them feel born clean, sterile / instill the terror of a narrow airplane escape from savagery / where their parents fell in love / where they met within tyranny / they can't read lolita in tehran / cut / embrace resilience as an american value / add suspenseful drums as militant iranians seek passports / add line: *here you don't speak english / here you're not welcome* / ben, show some fucking emotion / make the audience feel unsafe, feel estranged, immersed in badlands, scared / make them feel cultured in the history of Bad Brown Men / sophisticated in global affairs / grateful of their language / boast box office figures to a spiteful regime / roll out the red carpet / screen an oscar contender / tell the iranian actors quiet in the theatre / roll credits / watch how we liberate them

The taste of *taarof* is likened to my friend
Morgan's cock, hard in deference to our social
rank. *Taarof nakkon* I whisper as he puts me
in his mouth. In Iranian culture, it's an insult
to sit with your back facing someone. Immediately,
you apologize and touch yourself, timid
on your best friend's bed.

Taarof is a form of civility, an etiquette
of not being too eager, of promoting equality.
When one man's ritual is your desire, it's rude
to accept what you secretly want. Deny it
once. Deny it twice. Then put Morgan
in your mouth for your first time.

My relatives sip Earl Grey with a semblance
of apathy. *Taarof nemeekohnam*, I promise
I want to try this. *Taarof* can be seen as a plastic
denial of truth. Raisi touted Iran has no homosexuals -
and those who were in public, died, like the President,
by helicopter. To say "thank you,"

you say *dastet dard nakoné*: may your hand
not hurt. With Morgan, mine did. The polite response—
may your head not hurt. I wear Persian etiquette
like a silk veil, unraveling gentle *taarof* with each
taste of sin.

13 **persian boy**

no but what's ur real name?
my persian boi r u ok?
did u get screened at tsa?
i watched aladdin as a kid
i dream of ur magic carpet
i'll paint my face and b jasmin
ur culture is the culture of all the middle east
not a vulture lol i just love ur food
persian boy i love u

I woke up this morning hearing the Shema like I used to as a child. The caustic voices of singing soldiers in a desecrated Jenin Mosque, the prayer besieged.

In the story of Chanukah, a small quantity of oil used to light the first temple's Menorah miraculously burned for eight days. I saw an airstrike flaring over Gaza that they called "the fourth Chanukah candle."

I scroll All Eyes of Rafah CGI as another refugee camp is set aflame. It's unholy to extinguish candles yet kitchen sink cities still fall victim to our third degree burns. The first time I lit the candle, I was told not to walk through Gaza's slums. My curiosity drove me to a bazaar of smiles ancient in their warmth. I bordered a tarnished cartography etched into my sin and blew out candles when I saw a mosque pure as crosshairs. That night the absinthe tasted sweet in my vomit.

The ninth candle, the shamash, is a divine candle used to light the others. Last Chanukah, the largest Menorah in Oakland was vandalized and thrown into Lake Merritt, inspiring hundreds of Jews, Muslims, and others to hold candles in a vigil.

I remember when I let the Menorah's fire burn me when I was 18. *You're not supposed to put out the candles yourself*, they said on Birthright. *I thought you were a terrorist*, they told me when my beard grew. Years later, three Israeli hostages were killed after being mistaken for Palestinians.

15 The Menorah is extinguished starting from the lights on the left to the right, putting out various worlds in succession. Traditionally, Jewish rituals were celebrated by ceasing all of the fires and leaving only the shamash lit. Only at the end, everything was lit up again.

There's no tenth candle. You need ten men for a minyan to ascend souls higher towards heaven. I stand with nine others at my father's wake as I pray for him while facing the opposite direction.

baptized by the purity of her mother's heels
she longs to purchase white poppies
with stems skinny as brothers
growing ill from water poisoned
to drown terror or breath

snake charmers
forbidden from her gaze
still razieh is centered in the crowd
a cobra's eyes on coins
like territory
snatching money from an unscrupulous young girl
crying with a rock in her hand
angry as chamomile
as men mock bleached poppies
that grow from the mouth of the serpine
who fang her
insidious as self defense

again venom will spread to her brothers
as red everlastings in bright jenin fields
held captive in the deadnettles of wounds
that spread malignant over skies
shared by persians who deify goldfish the same
white balloons uprise from craters

confined in storm grates
among worrybirds & chewing gum
glued to the end of white poppies
planted in tarmac
razieh as in tranquil
sleeping in anemone invasive as life

17 vertigo's theory

neem oil mists
on falling aphids
making aseptic rooms
soft and redolent
like anti-wrinkle cream
on concrete
covered persian rugs
i kiss airborne mold
everytime you leave

saffron oil
repels basmati
served by a widow
to insipid men
sipping earl gray
stained and steeped
in arsenic
gowns turned compost
dense in seedlings
i smile
everytime they leave

mother sits
skinny and fragrant
as auburn walls
crumble like *tachin*
or cable jumpers
splashing a rear-view iris
arms splay as benches
awaiting rest
when toothpick bones ache
into highways
everytime we—

i've seen you here before.
where birds fall in vertigo to spool threadbare nests
and mercury pools mirror liquid iv tears
into isopropyl oceans you waded in a wheelchair.
time was never this centripetal.
now, contusions fog windows of my exit,
cavalier as hyacinth blooms to disinfect you.
feel the vascular exhale of blood pressure
when towns appear as apparitions,
stars as possible deaths.
lavashak wraps wrists like a bandage,
tissues sun-dried and sown in the morning.

a windless crow observes,
grows lilies from his face
everytime i leave.

Dandelion

The home I'm driving to is where my
mother won't arrive safely as the passenger
of my Nissan with airbags bursting like
dandelions, uninhibited and prolific on our
faces. The dashboard, a torn canvas where
I paint an emergency. Seat belts stretch on
craned necks leaving constellations on skin
like the rotting plums from my grandmother
who entered the world with no birthday.
Her daughter, that night, made it to the
hospital. She inherited four children who
drive her to the emergency room as
hometown conjugal visits. The first visit:
the collision of metal like the source of two
drivers screaming in silence. The second:
an airborne toxic event of the heart causing
peonies to bloom white. I can't hydrate her
trauma; the medics tell me it's not safe to
drink water. They will tell me it's my fault.
That night, we unbuckle and crawl out of
the car the way we stand up in synagogues.
The place she's driving me to—she changes
her mind and turns home after a temple was
bombed. On Mother's Day, I purchase a
bouquet of root vegetables to keep her cells
healthy. I give her fruit in a gurney. Sprinkle
vitamins on sheets. The bird feeder I bought
is overridden by squirrels and the finches
left her backyard. I think that migration
is a form of escape. My mother planted an
orange tree that no longer exists so I only
order fresh squeezed juice at brunch in San
Francisco where she's not invited. It washes
my mouth like cottonwood seeds. The home
I'm driving to is sheened in an ugly

moonlight that camouflages fireflies the
way we smile at funerals. Where Iranian
art molds in the garage and the backyard
awning falls into concrete. Here, the
oleaster grows with no purpose. Exiting
the car safely, I think of my father, who
grew petrified of the world outside his
garden, who refused to drive on mountain
roads and visit his doctor for blood work.
The place I've driven to now, my eyes are
sequined to the carnations outside the
window while I await her results. *I'm fine,*
she'll say as the casters roll closer, *go home.*

She woke,
a child wombed in ether
spitting mucus of theocracy
where gunshots wound the sky in Arabic geometry.

She grew
into a silhouette of shawls and chadors,
learned to decorate gestures on altars,
exhale Turkish espresso to men
staged on a vacuous altar
where false prophets openly carry.

A lineage lined with upholstered chadors
rotting in their naked offshoot.
She saw
generations of mosques used as weapons
in a firmament of gunpowder disguised as the stars.

She rested
in the harvest of black saffron crocus
& holy hymns muffled by hemorrhaging veils,
aperture thinning in the fingers of beasts.

Yet neither scripture nor lullaby nor morality police
could find virtue in that hideously breathing republic.

However she branches, the child
will learn to discern epiphanies from prayer,
one hand tattooed in prison; the other, fashions a bird's nest
of hair unclipped and wrapped in seraphim cloth.

Shawls blanket the kaaba
as a quilt stitched of bandages,
like goldfish, discarded in the sunset of eid.

So too do martyrs and bastards depart from departure,
from nightmares we pray no one will see as *azadi*.
She saw
light.

I stopped fasting for Yom Kippur several years ago. At some point, the fatigue became intolerable as I stared at office clocks in a malaise. I was the youngest child in Hebrew school to fast, perhaps seven. It was a silent competition against my yearning and my will. The younger I starved myself, I thought, the more I'd be unburdened by future sins. I'd be atoned for whatever wrongs that my selfish wonder would compel me to commit. I refrained myself in a vague, altruistic sense of solidarity with whoever else was suffering in the world. And the hungrier I grew, the more righteous I felt. There were no other children my age willing to devote themselves to this divine agony. I was a living Mitzvah. In this profound dialogue with God himself, morality knew no limits so long as I kept hungry.

Years later, my ethics incited me to defy an alleged homeland. I did so publicly in a series of viral social media posts that attracted praise and vitriol—both which inflamed my pride like a child starving himself. I spurred boycott lists and screamed poems to rooms full of nodding Jews. I emailed relatives in a tearful fury. I attended the occasional protest to post on my Instagram story. I drafted an anti-Zionist chapbook; sanitized grief into trauma porn. Affirmed others who shared a formidable hunger to split ourselves from the rest of our faith. Triaged artists to affirm my virtuous brand of another Jewish Voice for Peace. I shared my unsolicited art to Palestinian friends, taking off my keffiyeh to eat.

arcata to san francisco to nowhere
drifting in embryonic dusk
recall eyelids closing 'till acreage
turn miles turn oceans between us

each home splits us deeper like larva
or snake skin shedding
our veins reach other cities' sinks

can i remember
at nightfall when we woke
i thought the sky was my roof

now i roam drywall mountains vast as quicksand
and imprint chloroform on fresh wallpaper
just so I can sleep

recall
a love bequeathed from the past
turned gargoyle
while apathetic years cackle
in the mist

i almost forgot
how canines fight feral with prey
how predators hibernate
with flesh in teeth
before nomads grow hungry
and weave apart as gordian knots

i peel from one bed to the next in braille topography
hands strong as canary spines
intertwining with vultures
finding shelter in dross
disguised as marigolds

remember memory loss
how my wind is your solitary confinement
lungs carpeted in moss
breathing mold each inhale
fireflies afraid of light

every eleven years i shatter mirrors
and rest with scarecrows
rotting sugarcane the stench of home

i recall dreamscapes and nightmares
movement is a prerogative
nevermind my freedom
the condor's defense before flight

the ocean's false premonition of stillness

i recall home as gritted teeth
a garden all mulch
beneath sapphire eyes
pierced by armament clouds
footsteps decorate floorboards in exit wounds
cities blink themselves anew
a silent farewell lest i awake your stranger

macrame sheets bind legs to t o r n maps
sinews not in situ
a recollection fading
this time i'll rest regardless

this time i swear to call your breath my

own

Mothlight

Let's stay, they said to me last night. *I'm still here.* They stretch holes in my shirt and wedge the sun into them; close the curtains like eyelids in fright. Their name means famous warrior. Mine means righteous. I embrace the disillusionment the way last names are replaced but rarely spoken. The words *longing* and *love* are an interracial friendship. And I do wonder how to stay without grieving. How to give agency to the abuse of language. The thing about leaving is that it's more threatening than home. The thing about figs is they house dead wasps. Their name means fighter maiden. They'll arrange pathos across the floorboards and flood the apartment when I'm gone. *I'm growing a future in petrified oak*, they'll think. Sometimes inundation is a garden's only chance of survival. Their name means renowned. I'll arrive home to wool sweaters adorned in moths. The thing about home is the alocasias are infested—aphids breed on stressed plants. We'll sleep in flora stained in maggots and kiss them until our mouths are illuminated. Place detritus on perforated tape and wrap them around our bodies; parade with insects in our smile. Their name means illustrious—like the discerning of mothlight or wildfires in our rear view. The words *stitch* and *stay* are distant relatives. I watch them cut this poem with sutures, leaving each abstraction behind us. *Let's stay*, I said to them this morning, *I'm still here.*

this was never our home this was never
our home this was never our home
this was never our home this wasn't
our home this wasn't our home this wasn't
our home this is now our home this is
now our home this is now our home this is
now our home this is now our home
this is now my home.

I wonder how many octaves carry your
voice, how many melodies echo from
memory to fiction.

There are three octaves in a santur. The
first is the only time your hand struck me, a
nervous bass in your voice. We both stood
as burning coals awaiting the hookah's
inhale. Each lesson I've never taken pricks
my fingers like your wife's overgrown
weeds. Which is to say, my mother's lawn.

The second octave: a bellowing tenor in
Los Angeles. Which is to say, we only hear
you sing on cell phones. When my dog
was chased by a coyote, it was like all her
injuries healed. She sprinted with the vigor
of death. Years before, she slept beneath
the olive tree you planted to mirror the
sun. You stopped protesting her visits. after
we put her down, the cavity in our home
reddened like rust on samovars. The garden
turned to potpourri. I tried to occupy
space by crashing mezrabs on strings until
I disfigured my santur, the music cracking
like earthenware.

This is what you would have wanted,
which is to say myths.

The third octave was carried in your trembled voice when you told me to conceal faith. Which is to say, to be afraid of Muslims. To partition ourselves. After the 11th they scanned your gout for bomb residue. You never sang at the airport or at your cafe, where I helped position stars on Christmas trees viewed through prosthetic glass. We hung weathered lights like the brothers of Sultans, your fear mistaken for loathing.

Santur octaves are formed by 72 bronze strings tuned to ring independently of one another, like your brothers who decry home as a place of tarnish. When you sang, a migration of nightingales conjured revolution. I caress my instrument knowingly, as lipstick or Theocracy could have endangered us both. Which is to say, you kept me safe but never knew why.

There is an octave I sang to you once. I played my santur to frail eyes that pleaded in taarof, perhaps your only assent. Nodding to inharmonious melodies, you said broken strings croon better than silence. Rarely we spoke outside this music—an ephemera where your song was as aromatic as the lily you planted for me before you left.

And soon water spun in a crystalline vase
we used to make golab. To pour hydrosol
in earth. To accept the fading of skin into
the poppies that circumvented our faith.
Which is to say, we shared an inhospitable
and gorgeous melody the color of
rosewater.

Acknowledgements

Thank you to the soliditary of the Jewish anti-Zionist community in the Bay Area and internationally to inspire this collection, and to the brave leadership of Palestinians in their homeland and worldwide. Many thanks to my editor, and to artists and activists in community who inspire me everyday. Warm appreciation to my nearest and dearest and to my mother.

About the Author

Justin Ebrahemi (he/they) is a Persian American arts writer and poet based in San Francisco. *rosewater* is his second published collection of poetry, and his journalistic work has been published in KQED, Content Magazine, SFMOMA's Open Space platform, and elsewhere. Say hello at ebrahemijustin@gmail.com or on Instagram: @mr.babaaganoush.

Made in the USA
Columbia, SC
25 October 2024

44628816R10022